THE GREATEST CRICKET MOMENTS IN HISTORY

SVITEN KHAIRNAR

To my Parents

Bhushan Khairnar & Khushbu Khairnar

Contents

Contents

Foreword

Hi there!

First of all — thank you for picking up this book. Whether you're a cricket fan, a curious reader, or someone just flipping through the pages, I promise you're about to go on a journey full of sixes, surprises, and stories that will make your heart race!

My name is Sviten Khairnar, and I'm 11 years old. I'm a student in Class 5 at Crystal International Public School, and I play professional cricket for the Under-14 team. I've been playing cricket since I was just four years old, and honestly — I don't even remember a time in my life without it!

Cricket is not just a sport for me. It's a part of who I am. When I'm not on the field or in school, I'm either watching cricket, talking about it, drawing cricket stadiums, or writing down match scores (yes, even when no one asks me to!). My room is full of bats, balls, jerseys, and posters of legends like MS Dhoni, Virat Kohli, Sachin Tendulkar, Yuvraj Singh, and many more.

So why did I write this book?

15

The Greatest Cricket Moments in History

Because every time I see a legendary moment in cricket — like a last-ball six, a hat-trick, a flying catch, or a crazy comeback — my heart beats faster. I want to shout, "Did you see that?!" even if I'm watching alone. These moments give me goosebumps, and I never want to forget them.

I realized that cricket is not just about runs and wickets. It's about moments. Special moments that make fans cry with joy, hold their breath in tension, or jump up from their seats with excitement. Some of these moments become part of history, and others become part of our hearts.

So, I decided to collect the most magical, epic, unforgettable moments in cricket history and put them all in one book. This book is a tribute to those moments — and the amazing players who created them.

But let me tell you something else. This isn't a boring history book filled with only stats and numbers. Nope! It's a book written by a cricket-crazy kid (me!) who wants to relive those moments and share the feeling with you.

– Sviten Khairnar, Author. Cricketer. Dreamer.

Acknowledgements

Writing this book has been a dream come true, and I have so many people to thank for helping me turn that dream into reality.

First, I want to thank my family, who are always by my side. To my parents, thank you for supporting me in everything I do — from cheering for me at cricket matches to encouraging me to write this book. Your love means the world to me.

To my younger brother, Aditya, you're my biggest inspiration! Watching you become the youngest author in India gave me the courage to believe that I could write a book too. I'm proud to be your big brother.

A big thank you to my teachers at Crystal International Public School, especially those who encouraged my writing and always reminded me that my voice matters. You've helped me grow as a student, a writer, and a dreamer.

I also want to thank all the cricket legends who've made the game so exciting and unforgettable. Without your amazing moments, this book wouldn't exist!

To my friends and teammates, thank you for playing with me, supporting me, and sharing the joy of cricket every single day.

Finally, to every reader holding this book — thank you. I hope it inspires you, entertains you, and reminds you why cricket is the greatest game in the world.

This is just the beginning.

See you on the field!

ACKNOWLEDGEMENTS

– Sviten Khairnar

Author. Cricketer. Dreamer.

● x ●

What You'll Find In This Book

In the chapters ahead, you'll read about:

The day MS Dhoni finished the 2011 World Cup with a helicopter six and made the whole of India cry happy tears.

When Yuvraj Singh hit 6 sixes in one over — yes, SIX SIXES! — and reached his fifty in just 12 balls.

The time Ben Stokes pulled off the greatest Test match comeback ever, with only one wicket remaining.

When Anil Kumble took all 10 wickets in one innings, becoming only the second player in history to do it!

The wild 2019 World Cup Final, which ended in two ties and a Super Over, and left fans around the world totally stunned.

The fastest century ever in T20 cricket by Chris Gayle, who smashed 175* in just 66 balls — with sixes flying everywhere.

The moment when AB de Villiers became Mr. 360 and scored a 31-ball century with shots you'd only believe in video games.

But that's not all! I've also included chapters about the rise of T20 cricket, the amazing women changing the game, and even a bonus dream match — where I imagine all the legends playing together in one super match. (Spoiler: It's awesome!)

Sviten On Field

Sviten On Field

"This book is all about the craziest, coolest, most jaw-dropping moments in cricket history — the ones that made me jump, cheer, and yell 'Whaaat?!' at the screen. If you love cricket like I do, get ready for sixes, drama, and epic memories!"

ONE

Why Cricket is the Coolest Game Ever

Hi! I'm Sviten, and I'm totally obsessed with cricket. Not just a little obsessed — I mean cricket is life for me! I play it, I watch it, I dream about it, and I even write a book about it (you're reading it right now!).

So why do I think cricket is the coolest game ever? Let me tell you.

It's More Than Just a Game

Cricket isn't just about bat and ball. It's full of excitement, strategy, teamwork, and surprises. One moment a team is winning, and in the next over, everything changes! It's like a rollercoaster ride where you never know what's coming.

The Legends Are Superheroes!

I look up to players like Sachin Tendulkar, MS Dhoni, and Virat Kohli. They're like real-life superheroes with superpowers — only their weapons are cricket bats and brains. When Dhoni hits a six to win the match or Sachin reaches another century, it's like magic.

The Moments That Give You Goosebumps

There are some cricket moments that make you jump, scream, or even cry (yes, even boys cry during World Cup finals!). These moments are what I'm writing about in this book. They are unforgettable — not just for fans like me, but for the whole world.

Cricket is Everywhere

From the streets of Mumbai to the stadiums of Melbourne, people play cricket with tennis balls, taped balls, or even rolled-up socks. I've played cricket in parks, parking lots, and even in my living room (until my mom caught me!).

It's a Game of Dreams

Every time I walk onto the field with my team, I feel like I'm a step closer to my dream — playing for India someday. I imagine hitting a match-winning six in the World Cup final, with the crowd cheering and my name on the big screen.

So Why This Book?

Because I want to share the most legendary, unbelievable, and epic cricket moments with everyone. Whether you're a cricket fan or just curious, this book will show you why cricket is the coolest game ever.

So grab your helmet, hold your bat tight, and get ready — the greatest cricket moments are waiting for you on the next page!

TWO

INDIA'S 2011 WORLD CUP VICTORY – DHONI FINISHES OFF IN STYLE!

Imagine this: it's April 2nd, 2011. The Wankhede Stadium in Mumbai is packed with fans, and millions are glued to their TVs. India is playing Sri Lanka in the final of the ICC Cricket World Cup. The pressure is HUGE. It's been 28 years since India last won the World Cup. Everyone is waiting for history.

And then... BOOM!

MS Dhoni smashes the ball over long-on for a massive six.

India wins the World Cup!

The Buildup – So Many Emotions

India had played amazingly to reach the final. We beat Australia in the quarterfinal (Yuvraj was on fire!) and then Pakistan in the semi-final. It was like a dream! But the final was something else. There was excitement, tension, and even tears before the match began. Everyone wanted to win it for Sachin Tendulkar — the greatest player ever who had waited so long for this moment.

The Final Match – A Rollercoaster Ride

Sri Lanka batted first and scored 274 runs. That's a big score in a final. Mahela Jayawardene made a beautiful century. Then India started badly — we lost Sehwag and Sachin quickly. I wasn't even born then, but when I watch the highlights now, I feel nervous just like the fans must have felt that day!

But then came Gautam Gambhir and MS Dhoni. Gambhir scored 97 runs and kept India in the game. And Dhoni, our calm captain, walked in early and took control. He batted like a champion — no fear, no stress, just powerful and smart cricket.

That Winning Moment – Goosebumps!

And then... the moment that gives every Indian cricket fan goosebumps.

Dhoni was on 91 runs. Just 4 runs were needed to win. Nuwan Kulasekara bowled the ball. Dhoni stepped out and — SIX! The ball flew into the crowd. The stadium exploded. The nation exploded. And Ravi Shastri shouted on commentary:

"Dhoni finishes off in style! India lift the World Cup after 28 years!"

What. A. Moment.

Celebration Like Never Before

Everyone was crying — happy tears! Yuvraj fell on the ground. Virat Kohli and the team lifted Sachin on their shoulders and took a lap of honor. Kohli said, "He's carried the burden of the nation for 21 years, now it's time we carried him."

I wish I was there to see it live!

Why This Moment is Legendary

India won the World Cup after 28 long years.

It was Sachin's final World Cup — and he finally got the trophy he deserved.

Dhoni became a legend forever.

It united the whole country in celebration.

India's 2011 World Cup win wasn't just a victory — it was a dream come true for a billion people.

THREE

Yuvraj Singh's 6 Sixes in One Over – Boom Boom Boom!

Let me take you to one of the most explosive moments in cricket history — when Yuvraj Singh turned into a six-hitting machine and smashed six sixes in one over! Yup, you read that right — 6 balls, 6 sixes, 36 runs!

It happened during the 2007 ICC T20 World Cup, and it was one of the wildest things ever seen on a cricket field!

The Setup – A Little Fight First

India was playing England in a group match. Things were going great. Sehwag and Gambhir gave us a good start. Then came Yuvraj Singh, full of confidence.

But here's the spicy part — right before the over, Yuvraj had a heated argument with England's all-rounder Andrew Flintoff. It was like a mini-fight on the field! Yuvraj was super fired up.

Then came poor Stuart Broad to bowl the next over.

And Yuvraj let out all his anger... with his bat!

The Fireworks Begin – 6 Balls of History

Ball 1: Yuvraj steps across and flicks the ball over deep midwicket.

Six!

Ball 2: He moves to the leg side and smacks it straight over long-on.

Six!

Ball 3: He goes down on one knee and slaps it over extra cover.

Six!

The crowd is going crazy. The commentators are screaming. But wait — he's not done yet.

Ball 4: Another powerful swing, this time over point.

Six!

Ball 5: Full toss, Yuvraj launches it high into the sky.

Six!

Ball 6: One last swing — and it flies over midwicket into the crowd!

Six!

BOOM! BOOM! BOOM! BOOM! BOOM! BOOM!

The Fastest Fifty Ever

Oh, and guess what? Yuvraj reached 50 runs in just 12 balls — the fastest fifty in T20 history! That record still stands today!

He finished with 58 runs in just 16 balls. It was like a video game!

The Reactions – Mind Blown!

MS Dhoni couldn't stop smiling.

The crowd was dancing and screaming.

Stuart Broad looked shocked.

Even the England fans had to clap for Yuvraj's genius.

It was not just an over — it was a storm!

Why This Moment is Legendary

Only the second time in international cricket that someone hit 6 sixes in an over.

Fastest T20 fifty in just 12 balls.

Gave India a huge boost in the T20 World Cup — which we ended up winning!

This over made Yuvraj Singh a T20 legend. When people talk about power-hitting, this is the moment they remember.

FOUR

BEN STOKES AT HEADINGLEY – THE GREATEST COMEBACK EVER!

This is the story of a match that looked totally lost... until one man — Ben Stokes — decided he wasn't done yet.

It happened during the 2019 Ashes series, in the third Test at Headingley. England was playing against their old rivals Australia, and let me tell you — what happened on that final day was simply unbelievable!

England in Big Trouble

England had to chase 359 runs to win the match — which is super hard in a Test match. After two days of crazy cricket, England was almost defeated. They were 286/9. Just one wicket left. Game over, right?

Nope.

At the crease were Ben Stokes and Jack Leach — England's last hope.

Jack Leach is a bowler, not a batter, and he had to somehow survive while Stokes did all the hitting.

Stokes Turns into a Beast

Ben Stokes started hitting the ball like it was a World Cup final! He smashed six after six, playing fearless cricket. The crowd couldn't believe it. Every run brought England closer. He played reverse sweeps, powerful pulls, straight drives — you name it!

And guess what? He didn't stop. He kept going until the scores were tied... and then, with a boundary, he won the match!

That Last Wicket Stand – WOW!

Stokes and Leach put on a partnership of 76 runs for the last wicket. Leach scored only 1 run — but it was the most important 1 run in Test cricket history! He stood tall while Stokes went full superhero mode.

And the crowd? They went absolutely WILD!

The Reactions – People Lost Their Minds!

England's fans jumped, screamed, hugged strangers — it was THAT good!

Australian players couldn't believe what had just happened.

Even Stokes himself was speechless — but proud.

It was called one of the greatest innings in Test cricket ever.

Why This Moment is Legendary

England won by 1 wicket — the narrowest possible margin!

Ben Stokes scored 135 not out, under impossible pressure.

It was a comeback for the ages and helped keep the Ashes series alive.

People who saw it said it was like a miracle!

This match proved that in cricket — anything is possible until the last ball is bowled.

FIVE

ANIL KUMBLE'S 10 WICKETS IN AN INNINGS – ONE MAN ARMY!

Okay, imagine this: one bowler takes every single wicket in an innings. All 10. Not 2, not 5, not even 7... but 10! Sounds like a dream, right?

Well, Anil Kumble made that dream come true in 1999, against Pakistan, at the Feroz Shah Kotla Stadium in Delhi.

And that's why this is one of the greatest moments in cricket history!

The Setup – A Big Rivalry

India vs Pakistan matches are always intense. The fans are super passionate, and the players give it their all. In this match, India had scored a good total and set Pakistan a target of 420 runs to win in the final innings.

Pakistan started well. Their openers were solid, and India needed something big.

Then came Anil Kumble — India's spin wizard.

The Magic Begins

Kumble bowled with his usual focus and fire. He kept putting the ball in the right spots, and one by one, the Pakistani batters started falling.

1 wicket...

2 wickets...

3... 4... 5...

The crowd noticed something crazy was happening.

6... 7... 8...

Now everyone was standing. Could he really do it?

9 wickets...

And then... BOOM! Wicket number 10!

Anil Kumble had taken all 10 wickets in a single innings — the second player in the entire history of cricket to do it after England's Jim Laker (in 1956).

The Final Scorecard? All Kumble!

Pakistan: All out.

Kumble: 10 wickets for 74 runs.

Result: India won the match — but the real victory was Kumble's moment of magic.

The Reactions – National Hero!

The crowd in Delhi cheered like crazy!

His teammates hugged him like he just won the World Cup.

Even the Pakistani players congratulated him — they knew they had witnessed history.

Anil Kumble became a legend that day.

Why This Moment is Legendary

Only the second bowler ever to take all 10 wickets in an innings.

Did it against Pakistan — our biggest rivals!

He made bowling look like art and science combined.

It's a record that may never be broken by an Indian again.

Anil Kumble didn't just take wickets that day — he wrote his name in cricket's Hall of Fame.

SIX

THE 2019 WORLD CUP FINAL – A TIE, THEN ANOTHER TIE!

If someone told me a match could have two ties in one day, I'd say, "No way, that's impossible!" But guess what? It really happened!

Welcome to the 2019 ICC Cricket World Cup Final — the most intense, unbelievable, jaw-dropping match in cricket history.

The two teams?

England vs New Zealand, playing at the historic Lord's Cricket Ground.

What happened that day? Let me tell you — it was like a Hollywood movie... with cricket bats!

New Zealand Sets the Target

New Zealand batted first and made 241 runs. Not a super high score, but still tricky in a final. Henry Nicholls scored a solid 55, and the bowlers were ready to defend it with everything they had.

England's Chase – The First Tie!

England's innings had everything — a flying start, a middle-order collapse, and then... Ben Stokes.

He fought like a warrior. The pressure was HUGE. England needed 15 runs from the last over.

Ben Stokes hit a six... then came the most controversial moment...

The Accidental Boundary – WHAT JUST HAPPENED?!

Stokes dived to complete a second run, but the throw from the fielder hit his bat and went to the boundary! They got 6 runs — 2 runs plus 4 overthrows.

People were confused. Was that fair? But the rules said yes.

In the end, England made 241. That's right — the exact same score as New Zealand.

A tie in the World Cup Final!

Super Over – Round 2 Begins!

For the first time ever, the final went to a Super Over. One over each team. More drama!

England batted first — Stokes and Buttler scored 15 runs.

Now it was New Zealand's turn.

Super Over – The Second Tie!

New Zealand also scored 15 runs.

Two ties in one match! The world was SHOCKED.

But here's the twist...

The Boundary Rule – England Wins

The winner was decided by who hit more boundaries in the match.

England had hit 26 boundaries.

New Zealand had hit 17.

So... England were declared the World Champions — for the first time ever!

The Reactions – Total Madness!

England celebrated like never before!

New Zealand players were heartbroken — they played like champions too.

Fans all over the world were amazed, confused, and totally speechless.

Even people who didn't like cricket watched the highlights the next day!

Why This Moment is Legendary

First time a World Cup Final was tied.

First ever Super Over in a final.

Two ties in the same game — a record that might never happen again!

The boundary rule? It got changed after this match because of all the drama!

The 2019 final showed that cricket isn't just a game — it's madness, magic, and miracles all rolled into one.

SEVEN

SACHIN TENDULKAR'S 100 INTERNATIONAL CENTURIES – THE MASTER BLASTER!

If cricket had a king, it would be Sachin Ramesh Tendulkar. People call him the "God of Cricket," and honestly, I totally agree!

He played for India for 24 years, and in that time, he gave us so many unforgettable moments. But the biggest of them all?

100 international centuries!

No one else in the world has ever done it — and maybe, no one ever will.

What's a Century?

Just in case you're new to cricket:

A century means scoring 100 runs in a single match. It's a BIG deal. Most batters are lucky to score a few in their whole career.

Sachin? He scored 100 of them!

That's like scoring perfect marks in every exam for 24 years straight!

The Road to 100

Sachin scored his first century in 1990, when he was just 17 years old! That's younger than me!

After that, he just kept scoring — in ODIs and Test matches, at home and away, against fast bowlers and spinners. He scored centuries in every country where cricket is played.

By 2011, he had reached 99 centuries. The whole world waited for just one more.

Century Number 100 – The Moment

On March 16, 2012, against Bangladesh in an Asia Cup match, Sachin finally reached the magical number. He scored exactly 114 runs.

The crowd went crazy. His teammates hugged him. Commentators shouted in joy. And Sachin? He just raised his bat and smiled — humble as always.

Even though India didn't win that match, Sachin's 100th century was the victory fans had waited for.

The Reactions – History Made!

Newspapers had huge headlines the next day.

Social media exploded with "SACHIN 100*" trending everywhere.

Even rival players congratulated him. That's the level of respect he had!

Why This Moment is Legendary

No one else in cricket has scored 100 international centuries.

It took 23 years of pure hard work, focus, and passion.

It made Sachin a legend not just in India, but all around the world.

Sachin – More Than Just a Cricketer

He wasn't just about the runs. He inspired millions of kids (like me!) to pick up a bat. He made us believe that if you work hard and stay humble, anything is possible.

One of my dreams is to someday score even one century — and when I do, I'll remember the man who scored 100.

EIGHT

THE MIRACLE AT EDEN GARDENS – LAXMAN AND DRAVID'S STAND!

Let me tell you a story where the team was almost defeated. Fans had lost hope, the dressing room was silent... and then two batters walked in, held their ground, and created a miracle.

It happened in March 2001, at the Eden Gardens in Kolkata — one of the loudest, proudest, and most magical stadiums in the world.

The teams?

India vs Australia — and trust me, this was a battle for the ages.

Australia's Mighty Streak

At that time, Australia was the strongest team in the world. They had won 16 Test matches in a row! They were unbeatable — with legends like Steve Waugh, Ricky Ponting, Glenn McGrath, and Shane Warne.

India was struggling. Australia won the first Test of the series easily and now, in the second Test, India looked like they were heading for another loss.

Follow-On – The Worst Position

India batted poorly in the first innings. Australia scored 445 runs, and India replied with just 171.

That meant we had to follow on — bat again immediately, while still trailing behind. It's like failing the first round of a game and being forced to play again right away.

Everyone thought it was over.

But then came VVS Laxman and Rahul Dravid.

The Partnership That Changed Everything

Laxman was batting like he had something to prove. Smooth drives, perfect timing, total control.

Dravid, known as "The Wall," was calm, focused, and unbreakable.

Together, they batted the entire fourth day of the match. Imagine that — one whole day, no wickets lost, no fear, just solid cricket.

Laxman's Magical 281

Laxman scored 281 runs — at that time, the highest individual score by an Indian in Test cricket.

Dravid made 180 runs, and together, they built a partnership of 376 runs!

They turned a losing match into a winning one.

India's Comeback Victory

On the final day, Indian bowlers — especially Harbhajan Singh, who took a hat-trick — destroyed Australia's batting.

India won the match!

From follow-on to victory — it was one of the biggest comebacks in the history of the game!

The Reactions – Cricket's Greatest Fightback

The crowd at Eden Gardens went totally wild!

Experts called it "the turning point in Indian cricket."

Steve Waugh, Australia's captain, called it the "Toughest Test" of his life.

Laxman became a hero. Dravid became a warrior. And India believed again.

Why This Moment is Legendary

One of only three teams ever to win a Test match after following on.

Ended Australia's 16-match winning streak.

Showed the power of patience, partnership, and pride.

Gave birth to a new fearless Indian team.

This was more than a cricket match — it was a story of never giving up, even when the scoreboard looks scary.

NINE

Jonty Rhodes' Flying Run-Out – Superman on the Field!

Cricket is mostly about batting and bowling, right? But this time, it was a fielding moment that stole the show. One man ran faster than anyone, flew through the air, and made a run-out that looked like it came from a superhero movie!

That man was Jonty Rhodes — the fielder who made the world say, "WOW!"

The Scene: 1992 World Cup – South Africa vs Pakistan

It was a group stage match in the 1992 Cricket World Cup. South Africa was playing against Pakistan. The match was tense, and Pakistan's dangerous batter, Inzamam-ul-Haq, was at the crease.

Then came that moment.

The Run-Out That Shook the World

Inzamam tried to sneak a run. The ball was hit softly. Jonty Rhodes sprinted like a rocket, picked up the ball in one smooth motion… and instead of throwing it, he did something no one expected.

He launched himself into the air like Superman — legs flying, arms stretched out — and smashed the stumps with the ball in hand.

Direct hit! Inzamam was out!

Everyone watching the match froze for a second.

Then the crowd roared. The commentators shouted. And Jonty? He just smiled.

The Moment That Changed Fielding Forever

Before Jonty, fielding wasn't considered super important. But after that moment, everything changed.

Players started practicing dives, direct hits, and acrobatic saves. Coaches began treating fielders like match-winners. And kids like me thought, "I wanna field like Jonty!"

The Reactions – Instant Legend

The video of Jonty's dive was played again and again on TV.

Even his teammates couldn't believe what they saw.

Commentators said, "That's the best run-out ever!"

Jonty didn't just remove a batter — he gave fielding style and superpowers.

Why This Moment is Legendary

One of the most famous run-outs in cricket history.

Showed that fielders can win matches too.

Inspired a whole generation of cricketers to take fielding seriously.

Made Jonty Rhodes a household name around the world.

Even today, when someone makes a brilliant dive or a direct hit, we say,

"That was like Jonty!"

TEN

CHRIS GAYLE'S FASTEST T20 CENTURY – UNIVERSE BOSS MODE!

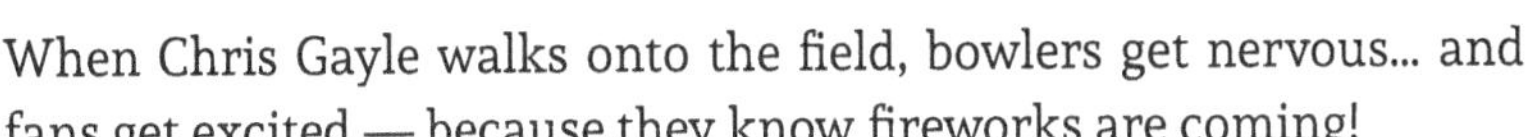

When Chris Gayle walks onto the field, bowlers get nervous... and fans get excited — because they know fireworks are coming!

In the 2013 IPL, Gayle did something totally insane. He scored a century in T20 cricket faster than anyone ever had — and he did it in a way only the Universe Boss could!

The Match: RCB vs Pune Warriors

It was April 23rd, 2013. Royal Challengers Bangalore were playing against Pune Warriors at the M. Chinnaswamy Stadium — a ground famous for big scores and big sixes.

But nobody expected what was about to happen.

Gayle Goes BOOM From Ball One

Gayle opened the batting and from the very first ball, he started smashing the ball out of the park.

6... 4... 6... 6... 4... BOOM!

He didn't stop.

In just 30 balls, he reached 100 runs — the fastest T20 century in history!

And he didn't stop there. He went on to score a mind-blowing 175 runs off just 66 balls.

Yes, 175 — the highest individual score in T20 cricket!

Records Broken That Day

Fastest T20 century – 30 balls

Highest individual score in T20s – 175*

Most sixes in an innings – 17 SIXES!

Most team runs in an innings – RCB scored 263/5, the highest T20 team total ever at that time!

The Stadium Went Crazy

Every time Gayle hit a six, the crowd got louder. People were dancing, cheering, and waving red flags. Even Pune's players looked helpless — they just smiled and watched the ball fly.

Commentators were laughing in shock! They kept saying,

"This is unreal!"

Why This Moment is Legendary

No one had ever scored a century this fast in T20 cricket.

Gayle hit the ball so cleanly and so far — it looked like he was playing a video game!

He showed the true power of T20 batting — fun, fast, and full of fireworks!

Chris Gayle didn't just bat that day — he exploded.

And from that moment on, he wasn't just a cricketer — he became the UNIVERSE BOSS.

ELEVEN

THE AB DE VILLIERS – MR. 360'S UNBELIEVABLE KNOCK!

What if I told you there's a cricketer who can hit a six over the keeper's head... while reverse-scooping the ball? Sounds impossible, right?

Well, that's exactly what AB de Villiers does — and that's why the world calls him "Mr. 360°". Because he can hit the ball anywhere — literally all around the field!

And his most unbelievable knock? The day he smashed the fastest century in ODI history!

The Record-Breaker: South Africa vs West Indies – Jan 18, 2015

The match was played at Johannesburg. South Africa was batting first. The crowd was expecting big runs, but no one imagined they were about to see pure madness.

AB de Villiers walked in after 38 overs were already gone. That meant he had only about 12 overs to play.

But that's all he needed.

The Fastest Fifty... and Century!
AB started hitting from the very first ball.
He reached 50 runs in just 16 balls.
And then hit 100 in just 31 balls — the fastest century in ODI history!
He hit 16 sixes and 9 fours in that knock. He made 149 runs off just 44 balls!
It was like watching a superhero with a cricket bat.

Shots from Another Planet
He reverse-swept fast bowlers.
He flicked full tosses for sixes.
He ramped bouncers over third man.
He smashed straight drives with one leg in the air!
Nobody knew where to bowl. The West Indian bowlers looked totally lost.

The Stadium Was Shaking
Every time AB hit a six, the crowd went crazier. They were screaming, dancing, and high-fiving strangers.
Even the commentators were shouting:
"This is ridiculous!"
"This man is not human!"

Why This Moment is Legendary
Fastest ODI century ever – 31 balls.
A masterclass in innovative, fearless cricket.
AB de Villiers showed the world that cricket can be both smart and stylish.
He became every kid's favorite batter — including me!

Mr. 360 – A True Artist
AB didn't just bat with power. He used creativity, imagination, and timing. That's what made him special.

Whether it was a reverse scoop or a no-look flick, you never knew what was coming next. And that's why no one will ever forget this knock.

TWELVE

M.S. Dhoni's Helicopter Shot – A Signature Style!

If cricket had a cool meter, this shot would break it!

The Helicopter Shot — fast, powerful, and totally unique. It wasn't invented in a lab or copied from anyone else. It came straight from the streets of Ranchi, created by the one and only Mahendra Singh Dhoni.

What Is the Helicopter Shot?

Imagine a yorker — the toughest ball to hit — coming at full speed.

Most players block it. But Dhoni?

He whips the bat with a full-arm swing, sending the ball flying for six... and the bat spins like the blade of a helicopter. That's why it's called the Helicopter Shot!

It's flashy, risky, and totally awesome.

Where It All Began

Dhoni learned this shot while playing tennis ball cricket as a kid. He had no fancy coaching back then. Just raw power, crazy timing, and a mind full of ideas.

When he brought it to international cricket — people went nuts!

That Iconic Moment – 2011 World Cup Final

We already talked about it in Chapter 2, but let's look at it again — the final over of the 2011 World Cup, India vs Sri Lanka.

Dhoni finishes off in style — hitting the winning runs with a massive six using none other than the Helicopter Shot!

That shot became instantly legendary.

Why the Helicopter Shot is Special

No one else played it like Dhoni.

It turned yorkers into sixes — almost cheating physics!

Kids all around the world started copying it (me too!).

Even big players like Virat Kohli and Hardik Pandya tried to master it.

More Than Just a Shot

The Helicopter Shot is like a symbol of Dhoni himself — cool, calm, and unstoppable. He didn't follow the usual cricket book. He made his own rules.

And that's why fans love him so much.

Why This Moment is Legendary

The shot helped win India the World Cup.

It became Dhoni's signature move.

It showed that creativity is just as important as power in cricket.

Today, if someone plays a helicopter shot, the crowd doesn't cheer for the batter — they cheer for Dhoni. That's how legendary it is.

THIRTEEN

THE RISE OF T20 CRICKET – FAST, FUN, AND FULL OF ACTION!

Cricket used to be a slow and long game — Test matches went on for 5 whole days! But then came T20 cricket, and it changed everything.

It made cricket faster, louder, brighter, and way more exciting — like a cricket match mixed with a music concert!

Let me tell you how T20 cricket took over the world, one six at a time.

What is T20 Cricket?

T20 means each team gets just 20 overs to bat — that's 120 balls.

So instead of playing for days, a match finishes in about 3 hours. It's like cricket's version of a high-speed chase!

In T20, batters attack from the first ball, bowlers try wild variations, and fielders make superhuman dives. There's no time to chill.

The First T20 World Cup – A New Era Begins

In 2007, the first-ever ICC T20 World Cup was played in South Africa.

India wasn't even expected to win — we had a young team, led by a new captain named... MS Dhoni!

But guess what?

India won the tournament in style, defeating Pakistan in a thrilling final. That victory made T20 cricket a global sensation!

Enter the IPL – Cricket Meets Entertainment

In 2008, India launched the Indian Premier League (IPL) — and boom!

It wasn't just cricket anymore — it was a blockbuster show!

Cheerleaders on the sidelines

Flashy jerseys

Huge sixes

Last-ball thrillers

Players from all countries in one league!

T20 leagues popped up everywhere — Big Bash (Australia), PSL (Pakistan), CPL (Caribbean), and more.

How T20 Changed the Game

Batting: Players learned new shots — scoops, switch hits, helicopter shots!

Bowling: Bowlers got creative with slower balls, yorkers, and mystery spin.

Fielding: Every run mattered, so dives and run-outs became match-winners.

Fans: Kids, families, and even people who never liked cricket started watching.

Legends of T20 Cricket

Chris Gayle – The Universe Boss

AB de Villiers – Mr. 360

MS Dhoni – The Finisher

Lasith Malinga – Yorker King

Rashid Khan – The Spin Magician
T20 gave fans new heroes — and gave players new styles.

Why This Moment is Legendary
T20 brought a revolution in cricket.
It made the game faster, more exciting, and more fun to watch.
It gave rise to new formats, leagues, and legends.
It made cricket cool for kids like me!

Now, when we play gully cricket in my lane, we don't say "Test match" or "ODI." We shout,

"Let's play T20!"

FOURTEEN

WOMEN IN CRICKET – BREAKING BOUNDARIES!

Cricket isn't just a game for boys — it's a game for everyone.

Over the years, women cricketers have shown the world that they can smash sixes, take stunning catches, and win matches with just as much passion, power, and pride as anyone else.

This chapter is all about the superwomen of cricket — who didn't just play the game, but made history.

Mithali Raj – The Run Machine
She's one of the greatest batters in women's cricket history. Mithali Raj has scored more runs in women's ODIs than anyone else!

She made her debut at just 16 years old, and in her very first match, she scored 114 runs! What a way to say "Hi" to the world!

She also led India to two World Cup finals and played over 200 ODI matches — a world record!

Jhulan Goswami – The Fast Bowling Legend

You think only men bowl fast? Meet Jhulan Goswami, the fastest bowler in women's cricket for years.

She took 255 wickets in ODIs — the most by any woman! Her bowling was fast, fierce, and full of fire. She even bowled out legends like Meg Lanning and Ellyse Perry.

Jhulan is proof that speed and skill have no gender!

Harmanpreet Kaur – The Big Hitter

In the 2017 World Cup semifinal, Harmanpreet smashed 171 runs* off just 115 balls against Australia. That innings is now legendary — full of big hits, powerful shots, and fearless cricket.

She plays with so much passion, it lights up the stadium!

And now, as captain of the Indian team and the Mumbai Indians (WPL), she's inspiring a new generation of girls.

Ellyse Perry – Australia's All-Round Superwoman

Ellyse Perry is the perfect all-rounder — she can bat, bowl, and even play football for Australia!

She once scored 213 not out in a Test match and has taken over 300 international wickets. She's one of the biggest names in women's cricket worldwide.

Smriti Mandhana – Stylish and Fearless

Smriti is known for her beautiful batting style and bold strokes. She was named ICC Women's Cricketer of the Year twice and became the face of Indian women's cricket for young fans like me.

She makes cricket look so graceful, and her cover drives are chef's kiss!

The Women's Premier League (WPL) – Game Changer!

In 2023, India launched the WPL, and it was a big moment for women's cricket!

Huge crowds

Big sponsors

International players

Non-stop action!

It gave women cricketers a platform just like the men's IPL — and it was AWESOME.

Why This Moment is Legendary

Women cricketers are breaking records and inspiring dreams.

They've shown that cricket is for everyone — no matter your gender.

Leagues like WPL are giving women the spotlight they deserve.

Girls everywhere now say, "I want to be the next Harmanpreet or Smriti!"

From dusty grounds to giant stadiums, women have proven that they belong in the world of cricket — and they're here to dominate!

FIFTEEN

MY TOP 10 CRICKET MOMENTS OF ALL TIME!

Okay, so I've shared a LOT of amazing cricket moments in this book. From Dhoni's six to Ben Stokes' miracle, from Yuvraj's six sixes to Gayle's crazy hundred.

But now it's time to choose my Top 10 Greatest Cricket Moments — the ones that made my jaw drop, my heart race, or gave me goosebumps every time I watched them.

Let's count them down!

---

10. Jonty Rhodes' Flying Run-Out (1992 World Cup)
The day fielding became cool — Jonty flew like Superman and hit the stumps.

Why I love it: Pure energy, pure awesomeness!

---

9. Chris Gayle's Fastest T20 Century (2013 IPL)
175 runs, 30-ball century, and 17 sixes — Gayle went full beast mode!

Why I love it: The most destructive batting I've ever seen!

---

8. Harmanpreet Kaur's 171 vs Australia (2017 World Cup)*
She smashed sixes like a boss and helped India reach the final.
Why I love it: A fearless knock by a fearless woman!

---

7. Anil Kumble's 10 Wickets in an Innings (1999)
The ultimate bowling performance — all 10 wickets against Pakistan!
Why I love it: One man, one goal, full domination!

---

6. AB de Villiers' 31-Ball Century (2015)
Mr. 360 broke all speed limits and played shots from another planet.
Why I love it: He made batting look like magic.

---

5. The 2019 World Cup Final – Tie + Super Over!
Two ties in one match. One winner. So much drama!
Why I love it: You couldn't script a crazier match than this.

---

4. Ben Stokes' Ashes Miracle at Headingley (2019)
One wicket left, and Stokes pulled off a miracle.
Why I love it: It was like watching a real-life superhero save the day!

---

3. Yuvraj Singh's 6 Sixes in One Over (2007 T20 World Cup)
Six balls. Six sixes. The world couldn't believe it!
Why I love it: Total destruction in just one over — and a record forever!

---

2. VVS Laxman and Rahul Dravid's Stand at Eden Gardens (2001)
From follow-on to victory — the greatest comeback ever.
Why I love it: A lesson in never giving up. Pure class.

---

1. MS Dhoni's World Cup-Winning Six (2011 Final)
"Dhoni finishes off in style!" – That six made history.

Why I love it: India won the World Cup. I've watched this moment a hundred times!

Bonus Picks (Because I Can't Choose Just 10!)
Sachin's 100th Century
Mithali Raj's record runs
The rise of T20 and WPL
My own first cricket match (Haha!)

Final Thoughts
These moments are not just part of cricket history — they're part of my story too. Every time I watch them, I feel inspired, excited, and proud to love this amazing game.

Maybe one day, I'll create a moment that makes it into someone else's top 10!

SIXTEEN

BONUS CHAPTER – MY DREAM MATCH (THAT I WISH REALLY HAPPENED!)

Okay, now that we've gone through the most epic real-life cricket moments, it's time for something special — a match that only exists in my imagination.

A match between the ultimate legends of cricket from all over the world, all playing in one stadium, in one mega final, with everything on the line.

This is my dream match. Let's go!

The Teams

Team A – The Masters

1. Sachin Tendulkar

2. Virat Kohli

3. Brian Lara

4. AB de Villiers

5. MS Dhoni (Captain + Wicketkeeper)

6. Ben Stokes

7. Jacques Kallis
8. Wasim Akram
9. Anil Kumble
10. Brett Lee
11. Lasith Malinga
Team B – The Titans
1. Chris Gayle
2. Rohit Sharma
3. Steve Smith
4. Kane Williamson (Captain)
5. Yuvraj Singh
6. Harmanpreet Kaur
7. Ellyse Perry
8. Rashid Khan
9. Jasprit Bumrah
10. Muttiah Muralitharan
11. Jhulan Goswami

The Venue
Eden Gardens, packed with 70,000 fans
Day-night match, under lights
Pitch: Flat and full of runs
Music, fireworks, and snacks in the stands!

The Match Begins!
Team A bats first.
Sachin and Kohli give a solid start.
ABD goes wild — reverse sweeps and scoops!
Dhoni finishes with a helicopter six!
Score: 212/5 in 20 overs

Team B chases.
Gayle hits 4 sixes in the first over!
Rohit plays a stylish 50.
But Kumble and Malinga fight back with wickets.

Then comes Harmanpreet and Perry — they build a super partnership.

Last over. 12 runs needed.

Final ball: Yuvraj on strike, Bumrah bowling.

Yuvraj smashes it high into the night sky...

Caught by Dhoni at long-on!

Team A wins by 4 runs!

Player of the Match:

AB de Villiers for his crazy 72 (off 30 balls)

and one flying catch at the boundary.

Player of the Dream:

MS Dhoni, for leading the team, finishing strong, and being the calmest legend on the field.

Why I Wrote This Chapter

Because cricket is not just about what has happened — it's also about what can happen.

This dream match may never happen for real...

But who knows?

Maybe one day, I will be in a real match with legends — or maybe become one myself!

The End... or Just the Beginning?

This is the final chapter of my book, but for me, cricket is just getting started. There are still more matches to watch, more moments to remember, and more dreams to chase.

Thank you for reading "The Greatest Cricket Moments in History" — written by me, Sviten Khairnar, a cricket fan, future player, and dreamer.

About The Author

Sviten Khairnar is not just a young cricket enthusiast — he's already a professional cricket player with a big dream and an even bigger heart.

Born and raised in Ahmedabad, India, Sviten is currently a bright and energetic student of Class 5 at Crystal International Public School. He plays for the Under-14 cricket team and has been holding a bat since he was just 4 years old! His journey began in dusty fields and small matches, but his passion, discipline, and love for the game have taken him to competitive-level cricket at a very young age.

Sviten wears the jersey number 27, which is also his favorite number, and proudly represents it every time he walks onto the field. Whether he's batting, bowling, or fielding, he plays with all his heart — just like the cricket heroes he's written about in this book.

When he's not smashing sixes or taking wickets, Sviten loves to travel to natural places, surrounded by greenery, hills, rivers, and fresh air. He has a deep love for animals and dreams of exploring the wild and protecting nature. Another thing he's crazy about? Superbikes! Sviten dreams of owning a GT Mustang someday and speeding down the open roads (once he's old enough, of course!).

Creativity runs in the family — Sviten's younger brother, Aditya Khairnar, holds the title of being the youngest author in India! Inspired by his brother, Sviten decided to write this book to share the moments in cricket that have inspired him the most.

With the spirit of a champion and the imagination of a storyteller, Sviten Khairnar is already on his way to making history — not just with his bat, but with his words too.

My Inspiration

This book is also special to me because of my family. My little brother Aditya Khairnar is the youngest author in India, and he inspired me to write too. If he could write a book, I thought, "Why not me?" So, I started working on this one — writing, researching, and reliving my favorite moments.

My parents, teachers, and friends supported me at every step. Even during cricket practice, when I came home tired, I still wanted to write because this book felt like a match I had to win.

Why Cricket Matters

Some people say, "It's just a game." But cricket is much more than that.

Cricket teaches us how to never give up, even when we're losing. It shows us how to stay calm under pressure, to believe in our teammates, and to respect our opponents. It's a sport that mixes skill, patience, passion, and team spirit — all in one.

For me, cricket has given confidence, discipline, and joy. It helps me focus in school, make friends, and chase my dreams. I hope this book shows you how powerful cricket can be — not just on the scoreboard, but in our lives.

Gallery

Enter Caption

Enter Caption

Enter Caption

Enter Caption

Enter Caption

Enter Caption

A Message To Readers

If you're a young cricketer like me, or just someone who loves a good story — this book is for you.

If you've ever jumped in joy because your favorite team won...

If you've ever felt sad when your favorite player got out...

If you've ever held your breath during a Super Over...

...then you already know how powerful cricket can be.

And if you haven't felt that yet — just turn the page. You're about to.

Thank you for joining me on this journey through cricket's greatest moments. Maybe one day, you or I will create the next big moment — the one kids will read about years from now.

Let's dream big, play hard, and keep loving the game.

– Sviten Khairnar

Author. Cricketer. Dreamer.